PAUL BUNYAN &ME
YOSEMITE

BY DEREK RYAN JENSEN

D1745588

Library of Congress Control Number:

2017905911

Library of Congress
US Programs, Law, and Literature Division
Cataloging in Publication Program
101 Independence Avenue, S.E.
Washington, DC 20540-4283

ISBN: **1533473803**
ISBN-13: **978-1533473806**

by Derek Ryan Jensen
Illustrated by Jimmy Pedron
Fonts by Kimberly Geswein

www.derekryanjensen.com
www.lucasfern.com

Dedicated to:

Mary, Garth, Gary,
Eric, and Raquel

This Yosemite Jr. Ranger Adventure book belongs to:

Jacob. ceda

Man is made or unmade by himself. By the right choice he ascends. As a being of power, intelligence, and love, and the lord of his own thoughts, he holds the key to every situation.

- James Allen

Contents

View from Glacier Point
Vernal Falls (Bottom) and Nevada Falls (Top)

Road to Paradise

The road to paradise was not easy for Lucas. It was full of sharp turns and steep cliffs causing Lucas to feel carsick.

His excitement for camping was quickly fading as he watched the world around him turn, just like his stomach.

His parents Talitha and John Henry Fern suggested he watch the road to feel a little better.

So far it wasn't working.

Lucy, his much taller twin sister was sound asleep under her favorite blanket next to Lucas.

It was not long before Lucas was so sick he closed his eyes and covered his mouth as his tummy began to give.

"Buuurrrp!" Lucas burped making a sound that was like hurling.

Lucy instantly flew across her seat as fast as she could, moving as far away from Lucas as she could.

"Holy cow, Mom! Lucas is getting get sick back here!" she squealed.

Lucas covered his mouth mumbling.

"I am not feeling very good!"

John quickly turned to hand him a small paper bag.

"We are almost there," John explained.

Lucy opened her eyes as wide as she could.

"That paper bag can't help!" she declared.

Lucas looked curiously at the bag before opening it up to look inside.

"Here he goes!" Lucy announced thinking Lucas was going to fill it up.

"What's it for?" he asked, looking over at Lucy.

Lucy tried moving closer to the door but she had nowhere else to go. If she pushed any harder, she would hurt her arm.

"It's for lunches," she claimed.

John turned to hear Lucy's explanation.

"What lunch?" he asked.

"It's to put your lunch back in it after you eat it," she clarified.

"Now I'm feeling sick," Tali interrupted, looking at Lucy in the rearview mirror.

"Just roll your window down," Lucy insisted. "The fresh air will make you feel better."

Lucas peeked inside the lunch bag again.

"There's nothing in my stomach," he

mumbled.

John looked over at Tali.

"Should we pull over for a few minutes?" he asked.

"I got this," she replied, turning on the GPS to show Lucas how close they were.

"You see!" John declared, "We are only a few miles away."

Lucas finally rolled the window down for some fresh air as he watched out his window for the Ranger Station.

He tried thinking of all the fun places his parents told him about going during their camping trip in Yosemite.

River rafting, bike riding, the Curry swimming pool, hiking, Junior Ranger exploring, and more.

After a few minutes, it started working. The more he used his imagination, the better his stomach started feeling.

Lucy was still worried about Lucas. She would not take her eyes off him, thinking he would explode at any moment.

"I see a building!" Lucas declared.

"This is Wawona," Tali explained.

"That's a strange name!" Lucy replied.

She saw the large white hotel in the distance, almost forgetting about Lucas.

"It looks like a beautiful place to stay," Lucas added.

"Funny you say that," replied Tali. "The Native Americans who first traveled to Yosemite Valley from Fresno named this place 'Pallachun' meaning a good place to stay," Tali explained.

A few minutes later they finally came around to the entrance of Yosemite.

"There's the Ranger station!" John announced.

"I SEE IT," Lucas shouted.

The car sickness scare was finally over, and Lucy was relaxed knowing that this long drive was over.

"Where is the camp?" she asked, looking

out her window looking for a place to park.

"The trees are wonderful!" Lucas declared.

John turned around in his seat to face them both.

"We are not at camp just yet! First, we will spend a couple of hours in the Mariposa grove, then we have another thirty-minute drive to our camp," he explained.

Lucas noticed a closed sign on the Ranger station window.

"Why is it closed?" he asked. "Do we need to wait?"

"No, we can drive right on through," Tali replied.

Lucy rolled down her window, allowing more of the cool morning breeze to fill the truck. Yosemite's heavenly scent was wonderful.

"I can almost taste pure oxygen," she said, closing her eyes to breathe it in.

Lucas immediately took a deep breath

trying to taste it too.

"I can't taste it but I can feel it," he explained.

Lucy saw Lucas make a weird face.

"Just stay on your side of the truck for me, please," she insisted.

John turned to notice the change in Lucas's face also. He knew that Lucas and Lucy were both gifted, but he had never thought his face would fill with light.

"What are you feeling?" John asked.

"You are lighting up like a light bulb," Lucy teased.

"I'm what?" asked Lucas, trying to look in the mirror.

Talitha was aware of the reaction Lucas was having. It was just how his body communicated with the trees.

"You're just fine!" Tali insisted. "Just stay in your seat."

Lucas closed his eyes and took a few deep breaths, and it was obvious that he was feeling something special.

"I just can't describe it," Lucas muttered.

Lucy looked at Lucas, puzzled.

"What does it feel like?" she asked.

Lucas tried harder to focus on what he was feeling.

"I don't feel sick anymore and I can feel that the trees are aware that we are here," he explained.

"Are you sure?" Lucy asked.

Tali looked back at Lucas in the mirror again.

"This connection is called ESP, and the feelings are only going to get stronger the older you get," she explained. "It's a good thing?" Lucas asked.

"You bring them hope and they are just letting you know that," Tali replied.

Lucas just closed his eyes wondering what kind of hope he could bring to a grove of trees.

Mariposa Grove

Talitha parked near an empty truck loaded with construction materials after arriving at the Mariposa Grove.

"What are they building here?" asked Lucy.

"They installing paths to protect the roots of the giant trees."

Lucas jumped right out of the truck to get a better look at the biggest trees he had ever seen.

"Holy moly, these trees are a thousand

feet tall!" he said.

John felt just as impressed, even though he had been there a hundred times before.

"These are the Giant Sequoia trees of the Mariposa Grove," he explained.

"Does Mariposa mean tall?" Lucas asked.

John laughed.

"No Lucas, it means Butterfly," he explained.

"I knew that!" he replied, leaning all the way back trying to see the very tops of the trees.

"How did they grow so tall?" asked Lucas.

"These trees are immune to everything on earth except lightning, fire, and people," replied John.

"How do they keep from being hit by lightning?" asked Lucas.

"They don't," John replied. "Many have been hit and burned or fallen. The ones we see today are the ones who have survived."

"That is sad," Lucas said looking at a giant

tree that had fallen to the ground. The roots were showing as if someone pulled it like a weed and laid it down.

Tali stood next to John. "Fun fact for you Lucas!" she warned.

"What's that?" he asked.

"Scientists have found that fallen Sequoia trees have lasted hundreds of years in perfect condition without decomposing," she explained.

"What does that mean?" asked Lucas.

"It means the trees are found fresh inside after hundreds of years. No termites or mold," she explained.

"Do you think it's still alive after it falls?" Lucas asked.

"What do you think Lucas?" she asked.

Lucas walked over and took hold of one of the roots on the fallen tree.

"This one does not feel alive anymore," he said sadly.

Unexpectedly a huge flock of butterflies flew by causing Lucas to take off running after them, almost forgetting about the fallen tree.

"Mariposa, mariposa, where are you going?" he chanted.

Tali walked over to where Lucas had touched the tree and noticed something strange began happening with the root he was holding.

Lucy interrupted as Lucas ran after the butterflies.

"There so many butterflies here!" she said happily.

Tali ignored the root of the tree, thinking it was just her imagination.

"Butterflies come here by the thousands during May and in June but most of them are gone now," Tali explained.

"Why don't we camp out here?" Lucy asked. "It's lovely."

"No one camps here," Tali explained.

"Not even you? You are Director of all the National Parks," Lucy said.

"Not even I can break this rule," replied Tali. "I wouldn't want to, this place is too sacred. People camping here would destroy the root system of these amazing trees within a year."

"I get it," replied Lucy.

"So, we only came here to bring Lucas to see the Grizzly Giant?" Lucy asked.

"Yes," John replied. "Then we will drive down and set up camp."

Lucas returned after chasing the butterflies resting his head against Lucy.

Lucy was bored.

"Why does Lucas need to see another tree?" she asked. "He can see them when we get to camp?"

"The Old Hara tree sent me to the Giant Grizzly," Lucas explained.

"Will he talk to you?" she asked.

"Trees don't talk," Lucas explained. "They communicate. You just need to pay attention to what they are telling you."

Lucas saw even more butterflies fly by and took off again running after them. Lucy's legs needed some running after sitting so long, so she chased after Lucas to wake them up.

John stood next to Tali.

"Even as twins, Lucas and Lucy are totally different people," he said cheerfully. "Lucy is much taller but more logical, and Lucas is much smaller but has a more spiritual understanding of Nature."

"Stay close, you two!!" Tali called.

Lucas grew tired of the butterfly chase as soon as a chipmunk passed, so he changed course and went after the chipmunks.

Lucy was already tired so she turned and ran back to Tali and John.

She was startled after noticing hundreds of Steller's Jays gathering above her in the trees. They had beautiful blue feathers.

A huge number of them came flying closer and closer to Lucy, totally freaking her out.

"What are they doing?" she asked.

"Take a deep breath," Tali insisted. "Nothing bad will happen."

The birds continued to gather and even fly right past Lucy causing her to cover her face from the wind they made with their wings.

"Awesome!" Lucas called out from a distance, as soon as he noticed the blue jays flying around Lucy.

Most of the birds landed right next to Lucy, looking directly at her.

"What do they want?" she asked.

"These are Steller Jays," Tali explained in a calm voice. "Some of the smartest birds on the planet."

Lucy was still covering her face and began peeking at them through her fingers.

"Why are they here?" she asked.

Tali smiled and squeezed Lucy tight.

"I have a feeling they are here to see you," she replied.

Lucy felt her heart beating faster.

"That's creepy! I thought we came here for Lucas?" she replied.

Tali giggled.

"It seems that Nature has chosen you too," Tali explained. "Why don't you try and find out what they need."

Lucas did not understand at all so he picked up a large branch from the ground and started running after the birds with it.

"Shoo, Shoo, shoo," he yelled chasing after them.

Only a few of the birds moved out of the way, but only a second before quickly returning.

Lucas was confused.

"My branch is broken," he said, throwing it to the ground. "Should I pee on 'em?" he asked with a goofy smile.

"Don't even think about it!" John warned, quickly picking Lucas up into his arms.

"Weee," Lucas yelled as John swung him around.

"It's a good thing I am small for a ten-year-old," explained Lucas. "Most kids my age are too big for this."

Tali placed her hand on Lucy's shoulder as she thought of what to do next. The birds were just chirping and waiting.

"Just relax and let them know that you care," she told Lucy.

Lucy looked at the birds and took a deep breath.

"Will they understand me if I talk to them?" she asked.

"It's like Lucas told you about talking to trees. You communicate through feelings," Tali replied.

Lucy took several deeper breaths.

"Calmly listen to the chirping. In your mind, you need to let them know that you care," Tali whispered.

Lucy closed her eyes and listened to the chirping sounds. Little by little, her heart found a connection pulling towards a little bird that was not far away from her.

She could see the bird in her mind and feel it was in pain. She could also feel it's mother nearby, including her sadness.

As soon as she opened her eyes she located a little bright blue bird with a twisted wing. The mother was next to it with the most beautiful dark blue feathers she had ever seen.

The connection to the little bird grew so strong, she began to feel a pain in her own arm.

"Oh no!" she cried. "What if it's broken."

Lucy immediately went over to the young bird and sat on the ground right next to it.

"You poor thing!" she said, wanting to pick it up.

Tali came up behind her to encourage her.

"Carefully put your hand out and wait for him to respond," she instructed.

Lucy slowly put out her hand and waited while the little bird looked over at its mother asking for permission, then it quickly jumped into the palm of her hand without delay.

Lucy's connection became so strong as she held it in her hands, tears began streaming down her face.

John Henry took Lucas closer to show him the miracle that was going to happen.

"I feel helpless. What more can I do?" she cried.

Finally, one of her tear drops began landing right next to the little bird in her hand.

"I am sorry, I don't know how to help you," she continued to cry, creating a tiny puddle in her hand next to the injured bird.

The little bird looked down at the tears and looked over at its mother again. After a few seconds, the little bird quickly drank some of the tears and quickly returned next to its mother.

Lucas saw everything.

"That's nasty!" he mumbled.

John immediately covered Lucas's mouth.

"No more karate comments out of you," he whispered.

Lucy stood up and wiped her hand off.

Lucas was still grossed out.

"She needs a baby wipe dad," Lucas whispered.

John tried not to laugh.

"What did I tell you?" he asked.

Everyone watched as the little bird looked around at all the other birds.

The wing still looked twisted, but within a few seconds, the bird started flapping, causing the twisted part of the wing to become straighter and straighter.

All the other birds began flapping their wings as a sign of support to the little bird.

"Fly!" Lucy called out.

Finally, the little bird lifted from the ground and flew straight up into the sky.

A few seconds later it returned with every Blue Jay in Yosemite creating a circle above Lucy.

Grizzly Giant

The hike to the Grizzly Giant took longer than expected after Lucas found a new love for hugging trees. Afraid he would never get the chance again, he wanted to hug them all, while whispering to each one how much he loved them.

"What a heart!" Tali said, watching Lucas do his thing.

Lucas ran up to a small cabin to read a sign in the window. It was the only building in the entire forest.

"Who is Galen Clark?" he asked.

"He used to live in this cabin and was called the protector of these trees," John replied with his big smile.

Tali gave him a funny look.

"Hey, that's my job," she teased.

Lucas walked over to the cabin and peeked inside a different window.

"Mr. Clark was lucky to live in such an amazing place," he said.

Tali spoke before John could even think of something to say.

"Galen Clark said that these trees looked as if they were giving us a warm welcome," she explained.

"He even wondered what these trees would tell us if they could speak."

Lucy was off in her own world, still thinking of the little blue jay.

Whenever she would stop walking she would look around to see if the little bird was somewhere nearby.

Finally, they made it to the king of all trees.

"Here we are!" John announced as they arrived at the base. "The Grizzly Giant!"

Lucas ran over and stood next to John, looking all the way to the top of the monster size tree.

"Holy moly!" he bellowed. "The branches look like bear arms reaching out to hug me."

"Then you better get over there and give him a hug." John insisted.

Tali went to keep an eye on Lucy.

John just sat to watch what would happen between the Grizzly tree and Lucas.

Right before Lucas climbed over the wooden fence, he stopped one more time to look at its giant arm-like branches.

"Is this really the tree the Old Hara tree wanted me to see?" he asked.

"That's right!" John replied, pointing to a part of the tree. "He's king of all trees, and I bet the best place to give him a hug is right next to that large burn right there."

"I see it! It looks like a giant scar, I bet someone tried to burn it down and then changed their mind," Lucas guessed.

"I'm glad they did, the world would never be the same without him," John replied.

Lucas studied the smaller scars carved out by visitors and even found a very sticky spider web under a large root sticking out of the ground.

Just as Lucas hugged the Grizzly Giant a rush of energy overcame him, pulling his thoughts deep into a place he had not been since the day with Old Hara.

Lucas felt the light inside the Grizzly Giant connecting to his own, creating words and even reading his thoughts.

"You are the greatest tree I have ever seen," Lucas told him as the connection grew stronger.

The Grizzly Giant had a light and energy that was even bigger than its body. Lucas saw the energy from the tree reaching all the way across the world.

"How is that possible?" Lucas thought.

The light became even more clear, allowing him to see how the energy and light of all trees and plant life were connected to people, in one way or another. In a way, it seemed that one could not live without the other.

The light of the Grizzly Giant finally gave Lucas the ability to share his own light and memories with the tree.

The tree was happy to meet such a wonderful human and felt happiness as it saw Lucas's happy memories. It also felt his pain and sadness during memories of pain or sadness.

It was like days had gone by as Lucas spent time with the tree. He completely forgot about his family who was waiting for him as he traveled through time watching the history of this magnificent tree.

Actually, Lucas was only with the Grizzly Giant for about an hour as John and Tali waited patiently for him to return.

Lucas learned more about trees than any person ever could in a lifetime. He even learned the Grizzly Giant's Native American name, 'No-taku-who-who-nau.'

Finally, Lucas remembered his family was waiting, almost breaking the connection before the tree stopped him. He saw one last memory that was different from all the others he had seen.

He saw a Giant Man standing right in front of the Grizzly Giant. He was almost as tall as the tree was.

"How is this possible?" thought Lucas. "Who could ever grow this tall?"

He also saw a blue ox who was almost taller than the giant man. The blue ox also had a large axe strapped to its back.

Lucas immediately knew it was Paul

Bunyan, the giant. His father John Henry talked about him so many times before, only he never imagined he was really that tall.

"Did he try to chop you down?" Lucas asked the tree.

A peaceful energy surrounded Lucas, telling his mind that Paul Bunyan was no longer cutting trees down, and he was out protecting them.

"Where is he now?" Lucas asked.

A sad energy surrounded Lucas, asking him to find out. The tree did not know.

The meeting finally ended as the Grizzly Giant gave Lucas a rare type of energy. An energy Lucas understood would unleash the full power of the Fern.

In time, he would understand what the power could do, and it filled every inch of his body. Lucas could feel, see, smell, hear and even taste the energy that was given him. Much more than he ever felt before.

The energy of the tree was curious to

know what Lucas was feeling.

Lucas thought for a moment before answering.

"It feels like rain, looks like fire, sounds like thunder, feels like raspberries, and it tastes like watermelon," Lucas explained.

The energy from the tree was full of laughter, as it faded away leaving Lucas to return to his family.

An extremely sad feeling came over Lucas as the tree disappeared It was as if he was losing his best friend.

Lucas opened his eyes to the sights and smells of the forest around him. He was completely worn out as he used all the energy he had left, just to move one of his legs forward.

John Henry was right there to catch him as he fell towards the ground.

Happy Isles

Lucas opened his eyes a few hours after fainting in the Mariposa Grove. He was left lying in his family's hammock next to their tent that was already set up. He was surrounded by hundreds of beautiful trees much skinnier than the Grizzly Giant.

The wind was blowing peacefully through the trees making a very soothing sound. Lucas felt like he was in heaven as he listened to the rushing of the river in the distance.

Right when Lucas noticed the swaying of the tall trees in the wind, his father John Henry came over, breaking him out of his spell.

"Welcome back!" he said booming down at Lucas from above. His deep voice was familiar and his smile was a welcoming sight.

Lucas looked around the camp.

"What did I miss?" he asked.

John began pushing him in the hammock.

"You lucked out, you missed the fun of setting up tents!" John replied.

Memories of the Grizzly tree were still fresh in Lucas's mind, especially his vision of Paul Bunyan.

"Paul Bunyan is here!" Lucas blurted out nervously.

Lucy laughed as she peeked at Lucas and John through a window in the tent.

"Lucas ate watermelon with Paul Bunyan," she teased.

"Did I talk in my sleep?" Lucas asked.

"A little," Lucy replied.

Lucy quickly zipped the tent window closed and started to come out, while Lucas looked up at his perfect view of the mountain everyone called 'Half Dome'.

Thinking of where Paul Bunyan might be, Lucas noticed the size of the cliffs around him.

"This place has hundreds of places Paul Bunyan could easily use to hide without anyone seeing him," he explained.

"It's nothing to worry about right now," John replied, giving the hammock another push.

"Can I have a turn on the hammock?" Lucy asked.

Lucas carefully slipped out of the hammock and held it for Lucy to climb in.

"Sure," he replied.

Lucy climbed into the hammock as Tali brought over a few folding chairs to sit and talk in.

Lucas was not wearing any shoes and felt the pine needles poking through his socks into his feet.

"They are not very sharp," he said moving his toes around.

Before Lucas could go anywhere, John wanted to make sure everything was clear about Paul Bunyan.

"Paul is my friend," he told Lucas.

Lucas looked oddly at John.

"When was the last time you saw him?" he asked.

"A few years before you were born!" John replied.

"How long exactly?" asked Lucas.

John thought hard for an answer.

"It must have been around five years or so before you were born, when he left for Ireland on a secret mission."

"That sounds cool!" Lucas replied, still a little doubtful.

Tali was holding the backpacks for their trip to Happy Isles.

"I met him!" Tali added.

Lucy was beginning to feel a little left

out.

"Are you sure you saw Paul Bunyan?" Lucy asked.

"Positive!" Lucas replied.

"I am confused," she continued. "Dad is John Henry, I know that. Stronger and taller than anyone I know, but that does not explain how a man can grow to be two hundred feet tall."

Tali felt Lucy needed a mother's view on the subject.

"You remember seeing how little Lucas was when he was born, right?" she asked.

Lucy remembered the picture of Lucas in her birth mother's hand.

"Sure. I guess that's right," she replied.

"Anything is possible," Tali explained. "Now let's get going before they close the nature center."

As soon as everything was closed and locked up, they began walking towards the bus stop.

"Paul lives in a large cave several miles above Muir Lake, near a glacier," explained John.

"Why didn't you tell us anything before?" asked Lucy.

"We weren't coming to see Paul," explained Tali. "Not until his giant ox, Babe, cracked the Hetch Hetchy dam."

"When?" asked Lucy.

Even John was unaware of this.

"Yeah, when?" he asked.

"I was sent the video this morning," Tali explained. "It's a good thing we were here right after it happened."

"What happened?" asked John.

Tali shrugged her shoulders.

"That is a good question, maybe you can help me find out," she replied.

"How does he keep from being seen?" Lucy asked. "I mean if he is two hundred feet tall?"

"He was seen for the first time this morning," Tali replied.

She pulled out her cell phone to show them a blurry video of a large blue ox with its horn stuck in the dam. A very large man helped pull it free before the video went fuzzy.

"This is Paul's blue ox, Babe. He was seen charging into the Hetch Hetchy dam yesterday," Tali explained.

"It looks fake!" Lucy noticed.

"It's not," Tali explained. "The people who recorded this video had their camera taken away by police right after it was sent all over the internet."

"So, what happens now?" Lucas asked.

"The government must protect Paul and Babe," she replied. "Just like they always have."

"That's good," Lucas said.

"Not really," John interrupted. "Lucas and I need to meet Paul and discuss what needs to be done," he explained.

"So far people might think it's a hoax like Bigfoot, but this video speaks for itself," Tali explained.

The bus stop to Happy Isles was not very far, but as soon as a bus arrived it was full of passengers, sitting and standing all the way to the front. With no room to even squeeze inside.

"I guess we are walking," Tali said happily.

"How far?" asked Lucas, worried he still might not have the energy.

"Only about half a mile," Tali replied.

Lucas was bummed about walking.

"I can't believe how many people come to Yosemite!" he complained.

"You are just tired," John explained as he lifted Lucas up on his shoulders. "Just a little more walking today, then we will be back to rest in camp."

Lucy did not mind, she just smiled and continued looking for wild animals.

The nature center was not crowded at all, and it felt strange after seeing a bus full of people going this way.

"Where did everyone go?" asked Lucas.

Another person interrupted from behind

them.

"Most people skip the Nature Center and just go on hikes up the mist trail to see Vernal Falls," she said cheerfully.

Tali smiled recognizing her dear friend Pamahas. A very well dressed Ranger with Ranger clothes that were spotless. She had beautiful long black hair braided under a large Ranger hat.

"Hi Pamahas," Tali said turning to give her a hug.

"Nice to see you, dear friend," Ranger Pamahas replied.

Ranger Pamahas went over to the kids who were waiting patiently.

"You must be Lucy," she said looking down at Lucas.

"I'm not a girl." he replied irritably.

Everyone laughed until even Lucas did when he realized it was a joke.

"I know," Ranger Pamahas replied. "Just making sure you were paying attention before we go out into the woods."

"I always pay attention," Lucas said standing straight up, looking around for anything he could use to prove it.

"I believe you," she replied.

Lucy stood in front of Ranger Pamahas to get her attention.

"I am Lucy," she explained.

Ranger Pamahas took her hat off to get a better look.

"What a beautiful girl you are," she replied. "Why don't you two call me Ranger Pam."

"That's much easier," Lucas replied.

"I rather say Pamahas, it's a pretty name," Lucy explained. "Where does it come from?"

Ranger Pam smiled.

"It comes from right here!" she said pointing to the ground.

Lucas looked for something special she might have been pointing at.

"I don't see anything," he said scratching his head.

"My name is American," she explained happily.

"What's is your name again?" asked Lucas, thinking he heard her name wrong.

"Pam-a-has," Ranger Pam repeated.

"It doesn't sound American to me," Lucas replied.

Lucy began to understand.

"She means America before it was even America," Lucy explained.

Ranger Pam reached out and gave her a big hug.

"That's right," she said, making Lucy feel important.

"Do you live here in Yosemite?" asked Lucas.

"I sure do!" Ranger Pam replied.

Lucas smiled feeling a little jealous.

"You are so lucky. I have never seen any place like Yosemite before," he said.

"It's because there is no place like Yosemite," she replied. "Every National Park is unique and each has a reason to need our protection."

Tali had something to tell Ranger Pam, so she carefully interrupted.

"Why don't you guys go and pick up a Junior Ranger handbook while we have a talk with Ranger Pam for a minute," Tali suggested.

Lucas took Lucy by the hand and started walking around the nature center. They saw many animals that looked real, even stuffed. The kind of animals that lived-in Yosemite.

A little farther away they found a real bear that was dead and stuffed, hanging from the branch of a fake tree inside the building.

Under it was a car door and a television showing a video of the bear when it was alive, breaking the window of a car.

"This is a door like the one in the video," Lucas said pointing to the door under the bear.

The door had no window and was damaged and bent, just like the door seen in the video.

"How sad!" Lucy said almost crying.

"The bear looks like it's still alive," replied Lucas. "It's so small."

John came over noticing a tear in Lucy's eye.

"Time to go outside to visit the fen," he said cheerfully, trying to avoid any tears.

"What's a fen?" asked Lucas.

"The fen is a small patch of wetlands here in Yosemite. It is a place bears love to visit so we need to keep an eye out and be safe," John explained.

"Maybe we will see this bear's family?" Lucas replied. "I want to see a live bear!"

Lucy was still feeling sad.

As they all walked towards the fen, Ranger Pam noticed Lucy's sadness.

"My grandmother's name was Lucy," Ranger Pam told her.

"It was?" Lucy asked, finally smiling back at her.

Lucy took Ranger Pam by the hand.

"It was her second name given by the

government," Ranger Pam explained. "She was called Pamahas like me before she was Lucy."

"I like Pamahas better," Lucy said. "I wonder if I can change my name to Pamahas."

Ranger Pam pulled Lucy and Lucas aside for a minute, in order to explain something very important.

"Pamahas means meadow, and as a Native American, the name is part of my heritage. It's who I am, so never be ashamed of your name, or who you are. Both of your names have an even bigger meaning than you could ever imagine," she explained.

"Like What?" asked Lucy.

"Your names mean Light or Light Giving. My grandmother taught me that," Ranger Pam explained.

Lucy was pleased with her name for the first time in her life. She always felt it was a little boring.

"I'm glad that I am Lucy," she told Ranger Pam.

"Do you have a last name?" she asked.

Ranger Pam smiled.

"I was an orphan like you two were before John and Talitha adopted you, only no one adopted me. I'm afraid that I don't have a last name to call my own until I am married, or legally take the name of my Grandmother," she explained.

"You don't need one," Lucy replied. "Pamahas is better than any first or last name."

"I think you're right," Ranger Pam replied.

Lucas looked around the fen as they began to cross a wooden path over water. The amazing bugs and birds made him more excited than ever. He watched a bug flying right in front of him moving its wings a million miles an hour, and it did not move. It would lurch back and forth in a perfect line.

"That's amazing!" he whispered to himself.

He thought of touching before Ranger Pam took him by the hand leading him deeper into the fen.

"Let's get working on earning those Junior Ranger badges," she said joyfully.

"Great idea!" Lucy replied.

Elmer!

As the sun was setting behind the tall granite cliffs surrounding the Yosemite Valley, Lucy snuggled up in a warm blanket while lying on the hammock.

She had her pink flashlight in one hand and was writing songs with the other.

Lucas helped John build a campfire to make s'mores.

Campers in all the other campsites were

returning from their different activities around Yosemite. Some were beginning to build fires of their own, while others were playing guitars and singing. Every camp was doing something different, as some people played games or started cooking dinner.

Lucas could smell the different foods and campfire smoke from every direction. The sights, the smells, and sounds were like nothing Lucas had ever felt before.

John Henry took out his large hammer and carefully split some wood for the fire.

"Why don't you use an axe?" asked Lucas.

John smiled and quickly put the axe away in his truck.

"That old hammer is my oldest and most trustworthy tool. I just pull it out once and a while to remind myself of the battles we've fought together long ago," he replied.

Lucas would love to hear his dad tell stories about some of these battles, but went back to putting marshmallows on a stick for toasting. Tali did not agree with some of the stories he told.

"I could live like this forever," he told his dad joyfully.

John laughed while picking up a stick.

"Hand me one of those marshmallows, would ya?" he asked.

Lucas tossed a marshmallow to John and watched him carefully poke the stick in one end.

"It sure is a great feeling to be out in such a beautiful place, with the best views on earth," John explained.

The campfire was now getting big sending smoke right into Lucas's face.

"I better move my seat," he said. "I promised Mom I would never smoke."

John laughed when he noticed how serious Lucas was.

"That was a great promise," he replied. This world has enough pollution already for us to go feeding even more into our lungs."

Lucas started to cough as the smoke

from the fire began to follow him once more.

"What's wrong with our fire?" he asked. "It's following me."

As soon as Lucas moved his seat to the other side of the fire pit, the flames began to send smoke right to where he was.

"I think the fire is in love with you!" John said, lowering his marshmallow into the heat.

"I am starting to smell like smoke," Lucas replied. "Mom might think I was smoking."

As soon as Lucas put his own marshmallow on a stick, the smoke went away.

"Why didn't I think of that before?" Lucas asked himself.

John just sat back and enjoyed the company of his little boy.

Tali was gone, helping Ranger Pam with a presentation in the Lower Pines camp theater.

Before any warning, an alarming cry echoed from the other side of the campground.

"EL-MER!" the voice called out.

Lucas sat up quickly in his chair.

Immediately another voice from the other side of the camp called out the same thing, only much louder.

"ELL-MERRR!!"

Now Lucy was the one to sit up in the hammock, putting down her Jr. Ranger book. She waited to see what all the racket was for.

"For Pete's sake!" she thought. "I wonder if someone is lost?"

Once again, more shouting returned, coming from everywhere. Even across the river.

Lucas started to feel so excited about the shouting, he stood up and started skipping around the campfire circle.

"Hey John," he called.

John was just putting the toasted marshmallow inside a graham cracker with some chocolate.

"Yes," he replied.

Lucas stopped skipping and began staring at the chocolate melting over the cracker.

"Why is everyone yelling for someone named Elmer?" he asked without taking his eyes off John's s'more.

"Calling out for Elmer has been a tradition for campers here in Yosemite, ever since the 1960's," John explained. "Everyone who camps here shouts for Elmer when the sun is setting!"

"Can I call for him?" asked Lucas.

"Of course," John replied. "This trip would not be complete without shouting Elmer."

Lucas took one last look at John's s'more, almost drooling. Then he let out all the air he had in his lungs.

"ELLLL-MERRR!"

Lucy came running over as fast as she could, almost tripping over the box of firewood.

"What is your problem Lucas?" she whispered.

Lucas shouted again before Lucy knew what hit her.

"ELLL-MERRR!"

John was laughing so hard, he almost fell

to the ground as he watched Lucy take off running for the tent.

"It's okay!" he tried calling out, but it was too hard to laugh and breathe at the same time.

It was too late. Lucy was already in the tent and inside her sleeping bag before Lucas could yell it again.

"This is great!" Lucas said, lowering his s'more cooker into the fire.

"Do you think we are going to see any bears?" he asked.

John put the entire s'more into his mouth, closing his eyes in delight as the taste hit his tongue.

"There is nothing better than a s'more by the campfire," he said as soon as he finished chewing.

"What about the bears?" Lucas reminded him.

John wiped a little chocolate off his face before answering.

"You only see bears in camp if you leave

out food or anything with a scent," he explained. "I have seen a bear unzip a backpack just to eat a tiny tube of lip balm."

"Gross!" replied Lucas. "I tried a little taste of Lucy's cherry flavored lip gloss and almost threw up."

"Bears love anything that smells. Even shampoo!" he explained.

Lucas wanted to change the subject so he could eat at least one s'more.

"Is Paul Bunyan really as tall as the Grizzly Giant tree, or was I just seeing things?" he asked.

After Lucas had such a long day, full of new experiences and information, John was excited to talk about his friend.

John looked over at Lucas, then he looked up at the top of the tree right behind him.

"Paul is about as tall as the tree behind you," he explained.

Lucas immediately turned around to look at the tree. It was the tallest tree around.

"That's really tall," he said nervously. "How did he get that tall?"

"He was also chosen by the Old Hara tree long ago like you were. But he did not keep his promise to protect trees. Instead, he found a job cutting down trees. With every tree, he chopped down he grew another inch," John explained.

"How did he ever stop growing?" asked Lucas.

"It happened after he made a new promise to the Grizzly Giant and finally kept it," John replied.

John looked up at the trees and paused for a few seconds.

"Paul has replaced every tree that he ever cut down, and has become one of the greatest protectors of trees the world has known," John explained.

Lucas yawned right after finishing his s'more.

"I like that story," he said feeling a bit

sleepy.

Lucy was finally out of the tent, now that the shouting for Elmer was over. She was hearing John and Lucas talk and was curious about what the trees wanted with Lucas.

"Why does the Old Hara tree and the Grizzly Giant need Lucas?" asked Lucy.

John picked up a pinecone and tapped it upside down, over the palm of his hand. Several flat shaped seeds fell out.

John picked up a little dirt and placed one seed in the center.

"Here, I'll show you!" he said, handing the ball of dirt to Lucas.

Lucas took the dirt into his tiny hands, cupping it tightly so the seeds would not fall out.

"What do you want me to do with it?" he asked while peeking in-between his fingers.

"What do you think these seeds are good for?" asked John.

"Seeds to grow a new tree," replied

Lucas.

"Now picture in your mind, the seed that I planted in the dirt you are holding," John continued.

Lucas closed his eyes and saw the seed.

"I can see it," Lucas replied.

"Now love it as much as you love the Grizzly Giant. Let it know how much it is needed here in Yosemite. Give it everything you got!" John said powerfully.

Lucas began to picture the seed become a little tree out on the edge of the meadow. He saw the sun come out and shine, giving light and life to the little tree causing it to grow taller than any other tree in the forest.

Suddenly Lucas felt a movement inside his hands as if a worm were inside the dirt John had given him.

"I feel it!" Lucas whispered opening his eyes and hands to see if it was really a baby tree that was moving.

"Look, a baby tree!" he whispered again,

standing up to show them.

Right then a huge group of campers shouted for Elmer all at the same time.

"ELL-MERR!"

Lucy immediately jumped, then plugged her ears.

"Why do they do that?" she said nervously.

Lucas smiled and found a large cup to hold the dirt with the little seedling. As soon as the plant was safely put away he took a deep breath, sitting right next to Lucy, ready to call out for Elmer once more.

"Don't you dare!" warned Lucy watching him very closely.

Lucas stopped just before yelling. Looking over at John he needed an explanation.

"Who is Elmer?" he asked.

John made sure Lucy was going to listen to the story.

"It was told, that a young man named Elmer was lost over sixty years ago. He lived here in Yosemite with his parents who worked at one of the large hotels."

Lucy plugged her ears as more and more campers began yelling for Elmer again.

John continued the story.

"One day this little boy Elmer became lost around camp so the family began calling out his name. As campers and hotel guests heard the shouting and understood a boy named Elmer was lost, almost every person in the entire valley started calling his name. It did not take people long to find him unharmed."

"I like that story!" Lucy said.

Lucas just wanted to shout for Elmer once more.

"Can we shout together?" he interrupted.

"Wait, there's more!" John said before continuing. "Later, it is told that Elmer worked here in Yosemite Valley selling fresh fruits and vegetables to campers. People would shout his name just like today for him to bring over his cart."

Lucy relaxed a little as the echo of people yelling Elmer continued in the distance. Now she understood the reason behind the shouting.

She felt almost as excited as Lucas now to call out Elmer's name.

"Let's yell out his name on the count of three," she insisted.

John did not hesitate.

"One, two, and three," he began.

"ELL-MERR," all three of them shouted.

Immediately another voice replied.

"WHAAAT?," causing all here of them to start laughing.

"Someone needs to go over and tell that guy the story," Lucy teased.

Little Bear.

Lucy was the first one awake in the morning. Her nose was sticking out of her sleeping bag feeling just how chilly the air was going to be as soon as she got out. The sound of the rushing river made Lucy need to rush on over to the bathroom.

The rest of the family was still asleep as

the sound of the river grew louder and louder.

Lucy quickly unzipped her nice warm sleeping bag and felt the chilly air rush in.

"My goodness!" she mumbled gritting her teeth.

She quickly found her clothes and jacket, finally changing out of her pajamas as fast as she could.

After returning from the bathroom, Lucy noticed how extremely peaceful and quiet the camp was. The perfect time for a bike ride.

She rode up to a large brown trash dumpster after noticing two short and furry black animal legs poking out of the dumpster door.

"Those are bear cub legs!" she said, riding closer to see if they were real.

She saw the legs moving and heard a familiar bear cub cry.

"Hold on little bear, I got you!" she grunted right as she took hold of the bear cubs legs, pulling it right out of the dumpster.

"Stop right there!" called a voice from behind her.

Lucy immediately froze while slowly turning around to see who it was. He sounded too young to be a grown up.

"Who are you?" she immediately asked, trying not to look him in the eyes.

She already noticed that he was around her age with and amazing smile and dimples.

"You can't just go pulling on bear cubs like that without getting attacked by its mother," he explained.

Lucy ignored his warning, still mesmerized with the cute young man in front of her.

"Hello!" he called, trying to get Lucy to listen.

Lucy felt the bear cub lick her hand, breaking her out of the boy's spell.

"I couldn't just leave it in the trash," she said keeping it from climbing back in.

"Why does it want to get inside?" asked the boy.

When Lucy pulled the bear cub away from the trash, the cub cried out causing a large 'BANG and a muffled roar to explode from inside the large dumpster.

"I think that's the mother inside," Lucy said, almost opening the trash door to look inside.

"STOP!" the boy shouted. "Now I know you are crazy. That bear could kill you," he warned.

"You're right," Lucy replied. "We need to find a Ranger."

The bear cub did not seem afraid of Lucy. Normally wild bear cubs just run away. This cub just looked up at her while sitting at her feet.

Lucy reached down and started petting it causing the boy to freak out even more.

"Who are you, the bear whisperer?" he asked. "A-AND You can't pet bears; didn't anyone teach you that as a kid?" the young man insisted nervously.

"I know!" replied Lucy reaching down to

give the cub a big hug. "I always wanted to do this."

"You can't hug them either!" he insisted nervously.

Unexpectedly a large garbage truck came around the corner to empty the large dumpster with the mother bear inside.

Lucy called the bear cub away from the road and began to wave her arms.

"Help me warn the driver!" Lucy told the boy.

The bear cub ran back over again trying to climb back into the dumpster.

The trash truck driver finally saw them and climbed down from his truck and to see why they were making him stop. As soon as he saw the bear cub he ran back to the truck to call for a Ranger.

The trash truck driver called and reported the bear inside the dumpster with a bear cub just outside.

The mother bear was starting to become

very upset, making mean noises and pounding on dumpster from the inside.

The boy took a few steps back, while Lucy stepped forward and put her hand on the side of the dumpster.

"That's scary!" he said. "Don't get so close."

Lucy tapped the side of the dumpster again to get the mother bear's attention.

"It's ok, we are going to get you out, and your baby is right here is just fine," she explained hoping the mother bear would understand.

The movement inside the dumpster immediately stopped.

Both impressed at Lucy's gift of calming baby and mother bears, the driver and the boy both asked Lucy the same question, at the same time.

"What's your name?" they asked.

Lucy giggled.

"I'm Lucy," she replied.

The driver seemed in a hurry, so he

immediately shook her hand.

"Great work saving bears today!" he said right before turning to leave. "You guys need to wait for the ranger and stay away from the cub," he added.

The bear cub was now rolled over on its back waiting for Lucy to scratch its tummy.

"That is amazing!" the boy said reaching down to scratching its fuzzy tummy.

"Don't pet the bear," Lucy teased.

"I'm Paul Jr.," the boy finally declared, standing up to brush off his pants. "I could not resist the cuteness."

"He said I saved a life," Lucy replied. "Why did he say that?"

Paul Jr. looked over at the dumpster.

"Right after each dump, the truck driver pushes a button crushing up everything inside," he explained.

"I am glad the river forced me out of bed this morning!" Lucy thought to herself while actually saying the words out loud.

"I've never heard that one before, how did the river force you out of bed?" Paul Jr. asked.

Lucy just realized what she just said.

"I meant, it was a good thing I got up early to see the river," she clarified.

The truck driver smiled and waved as he drove past the two of them.

Lucy and Paul Jr. began scratching the bear cub on the tummy. It kicked its legs as if the cub was ticklish.

"This may be the only time we ever get to pet a real bear," Paul Jr. said while breaking his own rule again.

Lucy smiled, knowing that she was the one calming the cub in her mind.

The bear cub rested its head by lying on Lucy's leg. "Hey there, little cub. We need to give you a name," she said, scratching behind its little ears.

"You can't name bear cubs?" he warned. "You will become attached."

Lucy looked back at him like he was crazy.

"I name him Elmer!" she replied.

Paul Jr. covered his face with his hands.

"You're hopeless!" he mumbled. "Now I'm going to think of a bear cub every time I hear people shouting that name."

Lucy pulled his hands away from his face causing Paul Jr. to look at her.

"Repeat after me!" she insisted.

Paul Jr. was not used to anyone touching him and was confused about Lucy's request.

"Repeat what?" he asked.

"When I am doing a good deed, I can, I will, and will not stop until I succeed."

Paul Jr. chuckled.

"That rhymes!" he celebrated.

"Just say it back to me!" Lucy insisted.

"I will not succeed until I bleed." Paul Jr. said as fast as he could.

Lucy laughed.

"No, that's not it," she replied.

"It rhymed, didn't it?" Paul Jr. joked.

Lucy repeated it one more time.

"When I am doing a good deed, I can, I will, and will not stop until I succeed."

Paul Jr. listened carefully this time, trying to impress Lucy.

"When I am doing a good deed, I can, I will, and will not stop, until I succeed," he repeated perfectly.

"You're a fast learner," Lucy cheered.

"Who taught you to say that?" he asked.

Lucy was proud to explain.

"My mom always says that if we remember to always be positive, we will not need to say I can't very often, and earlier you said I CAN'T, about five different times."

"I did?" Paul Jr. asked, feeling like an idiot.

"You-did!" Lucy teased. "Mom also taught me to do a good deed daily.

"How old are you?" Paul Jr. asked causing Lucy to blush.

"I am ten. Why?"

"You sound smarter than any girl I know,"

replied Paul Jr.

Lucy blushed even more.

Paul Jr. looked down to notice the bear cub asleep on Lucy's lap.

"There is something magical about you," he told her. "I bet you did something to put the mother bear to sleep as well."

Lucy looked over and realized that he was right. The mother bear was completely calm inside the dumpster.

"Do you know why Rangers tell us that it's not safe to pet bears or other wild animals?" Paul Jr. asked.

Lucy thought as hard as she could to give him a good answer.

"No," she replied.

Paul Jr. was excited to finally prove how smart he was to Lucy.

"Wild animals will feel comfortable with humans and start getting closer and closer to them. Eventually, someone will get hurt, and most bears are killed after hurting a human."

Lucy carefully set the bear cubs head on the ground before he said anything else. She just realized the danger she was causing this bear cub by petting it.

Finally, a Ranger with a ladder pulled up in front of the dumpster.

"It's Ranger Pam," Lucy said. "Come and meet her, she is amazing."

"How do you know Ranger Pam?" he asked.

Lucy stopped walking when she realized Paul Jr. knew her too.

"She is friends with my mom," Lucy replied. "How do you know her?"

Ranger Pam stepped out of the truck before Paul Jr. could answer.

"I would never have guessed that it was the two of you," Ranger Pam said cheerfully.

Her ranger clothes were in perfect order once again, perfectly ironed with her long hair braided perfectly into a bun behind her Ranger hat.

"Hi Ranger Pam," Lucy called.   Ranger Pam

pointed at the bear cub that was sleeping on the side of the road.

"What is that?" she asked.

"It's the cub that was sticking out of the dumpster. I pulled him out," Lucy explained. "The mother is inside."

Paul Jr. backed up, trying to avoid Ranger Pam.

Ranger Pam looked around the dumpster and found a little clip that was missing.

"What is that for?" asked Lucy.

"It keeps the bears from getting inside," Ranger Pam explained. "Someone in this camp did not put the clip back on after dumping their trash."

Ranger Pam was beginning to feel angry.

"Several bears have died this way," she added.

"I told her what happens when they get inside," Paul Jr. interrupted.

Ranger Pan turned and looked at him.

"What are you doing out this early?" she

asked.

Lucy noticed how strange Paul Jr. was acting around her.

"I was just riding my bike," Paul Jr. explained to her.

"Well, I hope you finished your chores," she warned.

Lucy started to giggle.

Lucy interrupted by tapping on Ranger Pam's arm.

"Is he your son?" she asked.

Ranger Pam looked at Paul Jr. causing him to blush.

"I am his nanny, but he calls me mom!" Ranger Pam replied.

"It's a long story!" Paul Jr. insisted.

Ranger Pam removed the ladder and started getting ready to help the bear out of the dumpster.

Several other Park Rangers arrived to help keep any campers from getting too close.

"You two need to go back to your camps!"

one of the Rangers insisted.

Ranger Pam paused to tell them one more thing.

"Finish your chores, Paul," she demanded, then looked over at Lucy. "I will see you later Lucy. Please tell your mom to call me when you return from the river."

Lucy waved goodbye and quickly jumped on her bike to ride straight back to camp.

"See you later Paul!" she called out without looking back.

Paul Jr. smiled and quickly jumped on his own bike, riding towards the wooden pathway to cross the meadow.

River Rafting

After breakfast was finished, Lucas made sure everything that carried a scent was put safely away, while Lucy helped Tali and John pump air into the river rafts.

Lucas noticed the life vest he was going to use was meant for a baby.

"Wasn't there a vest without a baby giraffe on it?" he asked.

John looked over to explain.

"It was the only one they had that will fit. Don't worry! You'll grow out of it before you know," he replied.

Lucas hated being so much smaller than Lucy. He remembered the time he had to wear a baby's suit and tie just to go to a wedding.

"I can swim, I don't need a life jacket?" Lucas claimed.

"Of course, you do! It's the law," replied John. "I am even going to wear one and I have been swimming for many years."

Lucas looked around hoping no one would notice him putting on the life vest.

"Dad, why would you need a life vest?" Lucy interrupted. "Didn't you out-swim the daughters of Nereus and Doris?" she asked.

Tali quickly turned to look at John, surprised at the stories that he had been telling.

"John Henry!" Tali teased. "What have you been teaching our kids?"

John simply scratched his head feeling just as surprised as Tali.

"I don't remember telling that story!" he replied. "I bet it was Pecos."

Lucas forgot all about his life vest.

"When do we get to see Pecos again?" he asked.

"He will probably show up one of these days." John replied. "You never know with Pecos Bill."

"Let's get going to the river. The water is perfect," Lucy insisted.

As they walked towards the river, John noticed Lucas started looking out into the trees, expecting to see something.

"What is it?" he asked.

"Do you think we will see Paul Bunyan today?" Lucas whispered.

John noticed how worried Lucas felt and stopped to take his tiny face into his hands.

"Paul Bunyan is the nicest giant you will ever meet," he explained. "He is my good friend and probably can't wait to meet you."

Lucas still did not feel much better.

"I just want to be prepared so I don't get too scared," he replied.

"That's perfectly normal, maybe later you can come with me to find him," John suggested.

Lucas felt even more nervous.

"Today?" Lucas asked.

"Yes, I need to go right after we finish our trip down the river," John explained.

Tali and Lucy were right behind them as they set their boats in the ice-cold water.

Tali lifted Lucas up and gave him a big hug.

"Ranger Pam says Paul Bunyan is excited to meet you!" she explained.

"How does Ranger Pam know Paul Bunyan?" Lucas asked.

"Rangers protect more than just National Parks," Tali explained. "Like your father, Paul Bunyan and his blue ox Babe are National

Treasures."

Without a warning, Paul Jr. came running up to the family as they were getting into the boats.

"Hey everybody," he shouted. "How far down the river are you going?"

"Who are you?" Lucas interrupted.

Lucy blushed nervously.

"This is my friend Paul, the one who helped me this morning with the bear cub," she explained.

"Paul Jr.," Paul Jr. explained.

Lucas couldn't help himself.

"A boy who is a friend?" he began.

"Please stop!" Lucy interrupted.

Paul Jr. began to laugh.

"Have you gone down the river?" Lucas asked Paul Jr.

"Not this week.," Paul Jr. replied.

"Can he come with us?" asked Lucas.

"He can if his Mom doesn't mind," John said optimistically.

Paul Jr. jumped into the boat next to John.

"She won't mind, this is going to be amazing!" he said looking directly at John.

"I'm rafting with John Henry," Paul Jr. whispered to himself.

Lucas heard him perfectly.

"Lucy told Paul Jr. that dad is John Henry," Lucas complained.

"It was my dad," Paul Jr. interrupted. "My dad told me."

John laughed.

"When did you see your dad?" John asked him.

Lucas and Lucy were beginning to feel left out.

"We just had lunch," Paul Jr. replied.

John was relieved to have Paul Jr. around, just in time to meet Paul Bunyan.

"Paul Bunyan is Paul Jr.'s dad," John explained.

Lucy slipped and fell off the edge of the

boat into the freezing water.

"What?" she asked sharply, trying to stand back up.

Lucas started to laugh.

"Why are you so small?" Lucas teased. "You were born small like me," he said cheerfully.

Paul Jr. laughed, feeling a little confused.

"Why were you born small?" he asked Lucas.

"That is something we are still trying to figure out," Lucas replied.

"Don't worry about your height, just enjoy any normal time you have while you have it," explained John.

Paul Jr. looked over at Lucas and looked back at John with one of the happiest expressions he had made all day.

"I still can't believe I am rafting with the mighty John Henry," he cheerfully whispered.

John laughed, while Lucas grabbed one of his arms feeling proud to have him as his dad.

"I love you!" Lucas whispered to John.

"I love you too, son!" John Henry replied.

Lucy felt confused and a little sad as they all pushed off into the middle of the river. Sitting behind her mother, she helped paddle the boat in a straight line.

The water was calm and it gave Lucy a few minutes to ask Tali a few questions.

"Is Paul Jr. going to grow tall like his father?" she asked.

Tali turned to wink at Lucy.

"Paul Jr. will be tall, but I think he would be much taller by now if he was going to be two hundred feet tall," she explained.

Lucy quickly felt relieved.

"How tall do you expect?" she asked.

"His mother is a mystery and it has been told that she can change her height to match the height of any giant," Tali explained.

"That's cool," Lucy replied.

In the other boat, the guys were beginning to hit the faster current in the water.

Tali could hear John's laughter all the way across the river as the boys tried to keep the boat from running into the bridge.

None of them noticed a very large person looking down at them from a cliff right below Half Dome.

Mirror Lake

Back at camp, it was Lucas and John's turn to clean up lunch as they prepared to meet Paul Bunyan. Paul Jr. watched Lucas with his father, wishing someday he could spend time out in the open with his own father.

Lucy and Tali were both gone helping Ranger Pam rescue an injured mule on the trail to Merced Lake.

The cold water had given Lucas a chill that would not go away, and he began shivering as the shade from the trees moved over and covered him.

John noticed his teeth chattering.

"Stand over in the sunlight and you warm up pretty quick," John instructed.

Lucas quickly moved back into the sunlight and raised his arms into the air trying to catch the heat like an antenna.

After a minute the warm light from the sun began to reach his bones. He finally stopped shivering.

"You're right dad, I'm feeling warm," Lucas said.

Paul Jr. led the way as hundreds of people were hiking to Mirror Lake. Lucas began to feel worried about how many people might see Paul Bunyan.

"Do you think these people will see your dad?" Lucas asked Paul Jr.

Paul Jr. chuckled.

"My dad can sneak up on a tiger," Paul Jr. explained. "He's an expert at hiding, both day and night."

Lucas felt relieved and was happy as soon as John Henry picked him up to put him on his shoulders.

"Your tiny legs are going to make us miss our ride," John explained.

They could hike much faster and make it to a hidden trail right past Mirror Lake, right inside the shadow of Half Dome.

The trail abruptly ended leading right into a granite wall.

Lucas looked up as far as he could see to the cliff of the mountain.

"We don't have to climb now do we?" he asked.

"Not from here," Paul Jr. explained. "Come sit next to this tree so you can see how we finish our journey."

Lucas looked around anxiously for any sign

of a giant man who is almost two hundred feet tall.

As soon as they sat down on a large granite rock, the ground began to move.

"What is happening?" Lucas called out. "Why is the ground moving?"

Paul Jr. could not help his laughing.

"It's just fine," he explained.

John took Lucas by the hand to keep him from running away.

"He is here," John said with a smile.

Lucas squeezed John's hand as hard as he could, pulling himself closer into John's chest to cover his eyes.

The ground below abruptly began to lift straight up into the air like an elevator.

"Are we moving, or am I just feeling dizzy?" asked Lucas.

Paul Jr. was enjoying every second.

"We are inside my dad's hand," he replied.

Lucas quickly looked around for some proof, unaware that they were now over one hundred feet up in the air.

"This is amazing!" he said, looking around at the world getting smaller.

He felt a tickle in his tummy as they continued to rise into the air.

Paul Bunyan's giant fingers curled up around them, keeping them from falling. Each finger was almost as big as John Henry.

Lucas looked up to see Paul Bunyan's smiling face. His teeth were hidden in the shadow of his thick beard, surprisingly clean for someone who could not use any regular toothbrush.

His eyes were giant too, with eyelashes that looked like whiskers of a giant cat.

"You are doing great," John said. "How are you feeling?"

Lucas did not even hear the question. He was still studying the largest human he had ever seen.

"This doesn't seem real," Lucas whispered.

Unexpectedly a giant rumble caused

Lucas to sit quickly on his father's lap. The rumble sounded like thunder was forming inside Paul Bunyan's chest.

"This must be our living LUCA," boomed the Great Paul Bunyan in his deep booming voice. "I love him already."

Lucas noticed that Paul Bunyan's breath smelled like peanut butter and jelly sandwiches.

"What is a living LUCA?" he asked with a shaky voice.

Lucas was bracing for more rumbling out of Paul's giant chest again.

This time Paul spoke with a lighter voice, avoiding any rumble.

"LUCA is the last universal common ancestor," Paul Bunyan explained.

"Don't give him any more reason to stay up at night," John Henry insisted.

"We can teach you about that later," Paul Bunyan explained.

Lifting his giant hand, Paul Bunyan turned them around to get a better look at all of them.

"Hey son!" he said once he noticed Paul Jr. was sitting next to them. "Happy to see you again today."

"I love you too!" Paul Jr. replied, pulling out his smartphone to play a game.

John Henry reached back and gave a few smacks on Paul Bunyan's giant thumb.

"It is great to see you again old friend," he said cheerfully.

"I miss your company ever since you came out of hiding, John Henry. How is that great wife of yours, Talitha?" he asked.

"She is doing better than ever," John explained. "Working on your case right now."

Lucas could not get over the overwhelming smell of peanut butter and jelly on Paul Bunyan's breath.

"Did you have a PB & J sandwich?" he interrupted.

Both John and Paul Bunyan began to laugh.

"Do you know why they really call them PB & J sandwiches?" Paul Bunyan asked Lucas.

"That's easy, Peanut Butter and Jelly." he explained.

Paul Jr. was even confused at why his father and John Henry were laughing.

Paul Bunyan finally explained.

"As one of the largest people alive, it has always been hard to eat enough food that will fill me up," he explained.

"Of course," Lucas replied. "You could probably eat a hundred PB & J sandwiches."

"That's right!" Paul Bunyan replied. "But back in those days, no one ever tasted one before your father and I came along."

"We started mixing the jam and peanut butter, and started a business selling sandwiches to railroad workers," Paul Bunyan said proudly.

John noticed that Lucas was still feeling confused.

"We named the business after the initials

of our own names. Paul Bunyan & John," he clarified.

Lucas could not tell if they were telling him a joke or not, but both began laughing as hard as they could.

The laughter of Paul Bunyan was much scarier than Lucas imagined. He was lucky Paul closed his fingers a little before anyone could fall out of his hand.

A distant sound caught Paul Bunyan's attention as he noticed a pair of hikers were on the hidden trail, getting closer to their location.

Paul Bunyan's eyebrows lifted giving him a slightly worried look on his face.

"If you don't mind, we must take this conversation to my home," he whispered.

John helped Lucas onto Paul Bunyan's shoulder to allow him to use both hands as he climbed.

Paul was quick climbing to the top of the steep granite cliff, holding on to trees and using large cracks in the walls to make it safely to the top of the cliff.

Lucas loved the ride as his tummy tickled with every lift.

It only took a few minutes to arrive at the tallest peak in the distance.

Paul Jr. continued to play video games on his smartphone, while Lucas studied the giant clothes and boots Paul Bunyan was wearing.

He was wearing blue pants with a red and white checkered shirt with giant buttons down the front. Each button was the size of a large pizza. His boots looked like the boots of a normal lumberjack.

"Where do you live?" Lucas shouted over the loud breathing Paul Bunyan made as he walked really fast.

"I have many homes in caves and hills all over the world." Paul Bunyan explained. "Right now, we will go to my home right below Mt. Lyell," he replied.

"We are almost there!" Paul Jr. interrupted.

John handed Lucas a water bottle. "Take a few sips to steady the effects of altitude discomfort," he explained.

A minute later Paul carefully lowered Lucas and John to the ground next to a small Lake with only grass and a few small trees.

"This place is beautiful," John said looking around at the endless views of mountain peaks.

"This is the Lyell Glacier," Paul Bunyan explained. "The main source of water to the Merced River you guys were floating in this morning."

The cool air reminded Lucas of how cold the river water was.

"I forgot to bring a jacket," he said as he started to shiver.

"It will be warm inside the cave," Paul Bunyan explained.

Lucas noticed he was barefoot the entire time, as Paul took one big step into the lake washing both his hands and feet.

He carefully walked over to a shady side

of the mountain full of rocks that were bigger than he was.

With the deepest voice Lucas ever imagined possible, Paul Bunyan spoke the password causing a giant rock-looking door to open.

Past the door was a large set of rock stairs for Paul, and a much longer and smaller set of metal stairs for normal size people.

The cave made everyone, including John Henry, feel as small as a mouse.

Paul quickly disappeared inside before the rest of them could even make it to the first step.

Home Sweet Home

Paul Bunyan's home was in a giant cave set up with furniture and other really big things. Paul Jr. even had a little bedroom in a smaller cave to sleep in on weekends or during school breaks.

Lucas was beginning to feel like Jack after climbing up the beanstalk into the giant land. Paul Jr. saw Lucas feeling nervous and knew exactly where to take him.

"Follow me," he invited

Lucas followed him to see what his bedroom was like, and as they were walking Lucas noticed the corral for Babe, the giant blue ox. It was in a darker part of the giant cave, only it was empty. The only thing inside was some fresh food that lined Babe's feeding box.

"Where's Babe?" Lucas whispered to Paul Jr., quietly, hoping Paul Bunyan did not hear him.

Paul Bunyan was talking to John Henry in the main room, explaining the situation with Babe at the Hetch Hetchy dam.

"They are talking about him right now, let's go listen," suggested Paul Jr.

Paul Bunyan seemed worried about Babe, and was wondering if the government decides he is too dangerous, what would they do.

"Babe left yesterday to find some apple trees to snack on," Paul Bunyan explained to John

Lucas could not resist.

"Do you just let him wonder?" asked

Lucas. "Aren't you afraid he might be seen?"

Paul Bunyan reached down and picked up Lucas and Paul Jr., setting them next to John Henry.

They all sat on a large table in front of Paul Bunyan. His deep voice caused the table to rumble, startling Lucas a little.

"Babe is old and wise," Paul Bunyan explained. "He's probably grazing near the Hetch Hetchy lake."

"Why did he crack the dam?" Lucas asked.

Paul Bunyan smiled and moved a little closer to Lucas. Close enough Lucas could smell his peanut butter breath again.

"We have both been a little upset about the damage the dam has caused to the Hetch Hetchy valley," he explained. "Babe is a creature of Nature and he wanted to do the right thing, only he did it without thinking of the dangerous consequences it would have."

"Did anyone get hurt?" asked Lucas.

"No, just a few feelings," Paul Bunyan

replied. "If Babe had really taken out the dam, thousands of lives may have been lost."

John interrupted.

"Babe understands the danger now and will help fix his mistake," he explained.

"Does he talk?" asked Lucas.

"No, but he understands," John explained. "The Hetch Hetchy dam is a touchy subject that affects the lives of millions, so millions need to decide its fate. It's not up to us."

Just then the smaller door leading to the top of the cave stairs opened and Ranger Pam walked in.

"Hey everyone!" she shouted.

She looked like she was a mile away, but for Paul Bunyan she was no farther than two large steps.

"Ranger Pamahas! It's great to see you," Paul Bunyan said welcoming her into his home.

He carefully allowed her to climb into his hand as he brought her down to sit next to us.

"What a treat to have so many visitors,"

Paul Bunyan said joyfully.

"I come with a request from Talitha and the President," she explained.

"The President of what?" asked Lucas.

Even Paul Jr. was a little confused.

Ranger Pam removed her Ranger hat and read from a letter that was found rolled up inside.

Dear Paul Bunyan,

The President of the United States of America requests the pleasure of your company for breakfast under Yosemite Falls. Thursday, July sixteenth at nine a.m.

Sincerely,
Chief of Staff
Brighton Carli

"That's tomorrow morning!" Paul Jr. protested.

"It sure is!" John Henry replied. "The path to Yosemite Falls is always full of people in the mornings, but I am sure security will make sure the area is clear."

Ranger Pam put her Ranger hat back on her head and looked up at Paul Bunyan.

"Talitha thinks you may no longer be required to keep your life a secret," she explained.

Paul's face immediately lit up with happiness.

"You mean I would be free?" he asked.

John cleared his throat.

"Don't get your hopes up too much," he explained. "There is usually fine print to read before you get too excited."

Paul Bunyan walked around the room and sat in a chair next to the large fireplace.

"I just am ready to stop hiding and live in a

normal place," he explained.

"No more secrets!" added Lucas.

"That's right!" Paul Bunyan replied.

John stood up and waived for Paul's attention.

"After learning about this Presidential visit, I think we need to get back to camp and prepare. Do you mind taking Lucas and I back to the spot you picked us up?" he asked politely.

Lucas began feeling a little sad. It's not every day a kid is able to spend time with a giant.

"Can't we stay a little longer?" Lucas asked. "Paul Jr. was going to show me how they get electricity all the way up here."

"It will have to wait," John replied. "I need to talk to mom and I can't get a signal way up here."

"Mr. Paul Bunyan, can I ask you a question," Lucas shouted as Paul was putting his massive feet into socks and boots.

"Yes, little buddy," Paul replied.

Lucas hesitated a little before asking his question. He wanted to spend so much more time with Paul Bunyan.

"I saw a cartoon once where you took the kids swimming. I know cartoons are not real, but I wanted to know if that ever happened?" he asked.

"It did, a long time ago!" Paul replied. "I take Paul Jr. swimming all the time, but no children have seen me publicly in over a hundred years."

"I am not sure if we will have time to swim here in Yosemite, but I promise to go swimming with you and your dad in the Grand Canyon, as soon as the dam is repaired," Paul Bunyan explained.

John looked up at Paul.

"Let's get going back to camp before we lose any more sunlight."

Lucas tapped Paul Jr. on the shoulder.

"How did Ranger Pam get here so fast?"

he asked. "She was just with my mom."

Paul Jr. chuckled.

"Search and Rescue are always making trips up here, so we usually just ask for a ride," he explained.

After everyone was securely sitting on Paul Bunyan's shoulders, Paul left his home to hike down the mountain to drop them off.

"Hey John," Paul Bunyan called as he continued to walk.

"Yes," John replied.

"When do you leave for the Grand Canyon?" he asked.

"Probably tomorrow after the President leaves," John replied.

"I probably will not make it for another few days, not until the crack in the dam is fixed," Paul Bunyan explained.

"We are going to need your help," John insisted. "Kokopelli is not easy to find, and if we find her, we will need your help to get her into the basket."

"Did we find the basket yet?" asked Paul Bunyan.

"My grandmother's basket is in my living room," Ranger Pam interrupted. "Safe and sound."

Lucas was completely lost.

"I thought we were going to the Grand Canyon to go camping," he told his dad. "And who is Kokopelli?"

John smiled at Lucas calmly.

"We are going camping there as promised. We just need to pick up Kokopelli to help us solve this climate problem we have been facing," John explained.

"Yes, but who is Kokopelli?" Lucas repeated.

John continued to explain.

"Kokopelli is very powerful and is usually resting between seasons. She controls most of the elements that give us wind, rain, and snow."

"So, is Kokopelli the name of Mother Nature?" Lucas asked.

"It is the name she has been called for over five thousand years," John replied.

Lucas finally understood a little better. He was still frustrated having to leave Yosemite so soon.

"Why do we leave tomorrow?" he asked.

John was expecting this question all day.

"We will be back next year," John said joyfully, "And tomorrow you get to ride on a train called the Cannonball."

Lucas instantly felt better.

"With Casey Jones?" he asked.

"The one and only," John replied.

Secrets

Early the next morning, Lucy woke up to the thunderous sound of a garbage truck dumping one of the large dumpsters of campground trash.

She was immediately reminded of the bear cub that was trapped the day before, so she quickly put on her clothes and ran over to make sure the bear clips were put back.

She was thankful when she saw the clips were secure and no bears could be inside.

A familiar voice spoke to her from behind.

"I already checked all dumpsters in your camp!" the voice called from behind.

Lucy turned as fast as she could to find Paul Jr. standing there.

"That was right out of the Jr. Ranger handbook," Lucy told him proudly. "A good deed for today."

"Yes, it was," Paul Jr. replied with a big smile on his face.

"Why are you up this early in the morning?" Lucy asked him. "Breakfast with the President is not for another three hours."

"I'm not invited to the breakfast, and my mom has a long list of things for me to do before leaving for Ireland this afternoon," he replied.

Paul Jr. looked down at the ground feeling sorry for himself.

"They left me out of the Grand Canyon

trip," he mumbled.

"That's terrible, why can't you come? asked Lucy.

Paul kicked his feet in the pine needles covering the dirt.

"My birth mom is in Ireland and I was told she needed me," he explained.

"Cheer up! It sounds fun," she said cheerfully, trying to cheer him up.

"My mother is a little boring," he explained.

Lucy was sad Paul Jr. was not going to the Grand Canyon.

"How did Paul Bunyan meet a girl in Ireland?" asked Lucy. "She must be one tall momma."

"She is tall when she wants to be, but that's a long story," Paul explained.

"What's her name?" Lucy asked.

Paul was not in the mood to talk about his birth mom. He felt that he hardly knew her.

"It is hard for some people to say," he replied. "Her name is Bébinn."

Lucy tried to picture a woman named Bébinn.

"That is a very pretty name. Do you have a picture?" she asked.

Paul felt embarrassed that he did not have a picture, and mostly because he could hardly remember what his mom Bébinn looked like.

"This may sound strange, but I am not allowed to have or take pictures of either of my parents," he whispered.

Lucy giggled.

"It's not easy for weirdos like us who have strange parents," she said hoping to make him smile.

Paul started laughing.

"My mom Bébinn is the strangest of all. Hopefully your family can come and meet her after the Grand Canyon," he replied.

"That would be fun," Lucy replied. "Is Bébinn nice to you?"

"She's nice, but she has a huge hazelnut

farm and she is hardly home to spend time with," he explained.

Lucy smiled and felt happy that Paul was willing to trust her with so much of his personal life.

Paul Jr. began noticing how strange the animals were starting to act. Blue jays, squirrels, ravens, and even a few deer began getting closer to them.

"This is kinda creepy!" Paul Jr. said pointing at a dozen ravens that just landed on the dumpster in front of them.

Lucy was calling them on purpose using her mind. She wanted to share her own secret with Paul Jr.

"If I tell you a secret, do you promise not to tell anyone?" she asked.

Paul looked around at all the animals listening quietly.

"I can keep a secret, but I think we have a few more ears that may not be able to," he replied. "Did you notice that none of the animals are making any noise?"

"That is my secret," Lucy whispered. "I can communicate with animals."

Paul Jr. looked over at the squirrels that were getting closer and closer to his feet.

"I did notice something strange between you and the bear cub the other day," he whispered back to her. "I just did not know it was this cool!"

"Do you want to see something else?" asked Lucy.

Paul Jr. looked up at Lucy already impressed.

"Go ahead," he invited.

Lucy knelt on the pine needles and dirt and closed her eyes.

For about a minute nothing happened until finally there was movement from every corner of the campground. Even more squirrels were running as fast as they could towards Lucy. They climbed down trees, out of holes in the ground and began getting a little too close to Paul Jr.

Paul Jr. scared away the ravens and climbed to the top of the dumpster faster than he thought was even possible.

"That's good enough." Paul Jr. warned.

Lucy started to laugh when she heard a voice calling from the bathrooms.

"Luuu-cccy!!"

It was her mom Tali, so Lucy quickly stood up and gently waved her arms at all the animals, sending them away.

"I'M OVER HERE!" she yelled back.

"Come back and start getting ready," Tali called back to her.

Lucy helped Paul Jr. jump down from the top of the dumpster.

"I need to go," she explained. "First, tell me what your dad is like. Lucas went to bed before telling me"

"It is still hard to believe that Lucas is your twin," he replied. "My dad is great."

"Lucas is a long story," Lucy replied. "I

can't wait to meet the great Paul Bunyan."

"My dad is big but he is not scary at all. He is the nicest dad a boy could have," he explained.

"Does he still love Bébinn?" she asked.

"More than anyone could love someone," Paul replied cheerfully.

"Then they will be back together before you know it," Lucy explained. "What time do you leave tomorrow?"

Paul began walking home.

"I catch the train from Sugar Pine with your family right after lunch," he replied.

Lucy was confused.

"Don't you need to fly to get to Ireland?" she asked.

Paul stopped walking and smiled.

"The Cannonball can get you anywhere faster than planes or boats," he explained.

"What's the Cannonball?" she asked.

"It's the name of Casey Jone's train," he replied.

"Sounds impossible that it would be faster than a plane, but I guess anything is possible in our world," Lucy said happily, before returning to her camp.

Paul Bunyan & Me

Lucas was relaxing in the hammock before it was time to meet the President. Right now, the President was finishing breakfast with Paul Bunyan and probably watching him eat a thousand pancakes. Every kid's dream.

It had been a few days since he saw the Grizzly Giant tree, and he missed the peace he felt when he was there.

He closed his eyes with the sound of the

river and the scent of the trees around him. He tried to relax and remember that moment.

Abruptly, Lucas felt himself being absorbed into the trees around him.

"What is happening?" he called out kicking his legs as if they were being held down.

The memory of the Grizzly Giant returned, calming Lucas until he was pulled inside the light of a thousand trees. They were under the direction of the Grizzly Giant.

"Where am I?" he asked.

The sound of water and wind filled his mind until he floated into the air without his body. He was pulled to the tops of the trees and could see his body below, lying in the hammock as if he were asleep.

He felt just as peaceful as he was with the Grizzly Giant, as he looked around and saw John and his Mom packing up some clothes.

"This is amazing!" he thought.

"Where is Lucy?" he questioned.

The branches of the trees began to

move, and with the help of a breeze, he was pushed towards her.

Lucy was right below him reading a book next to the river.

"There she is!" he said cheerfully.

Lucas called out to her trying to get her to look up.

"LUCY!" he called as loud as he could.

Lucy looked around hearing his voice, but could not see him. She continued to read her book.

"Where is Paul Bunyan?" Lucas thought, hoping to see what he was doing with the President.

After another gentle push of the wind, and trees, Lucas appeared directly over the breakfast table where Paul was sitting with the President.

It was almost over and Paul Bunyan was laughing at something the President said.

"This is the weirdest thing that has ever happened to me," Lucas said to himself.

Paul Bunyan heard Lucas but thought it was the President.

"What's strange?" Paul Bunyan asked the President.

The President looked up at Paul Bunyan feeling confused about his question.

"What do you mean?" he asked.

Paul Bunyan suddenly realized that it was the voice of Lucas, so he looked around the forest for his little friend.

Lucas snickered causing Paul to hear him and look directly at him.

Lucas realized that Paul could hear him but the President could not.

"Can you hear me?" he asked.

Paul squinted his eyes to get a better look.

"Is that you Lucas Fern?" he asked.

Lucas panicked and thought of the hammock where his body was sleeping.

"Lucas, wake up!" John called from inside the tent.

Lucas opened his eyes and looked for his father.

"What happened?" he asked.

Lucy and Tali were walking towards him.

"Did you have a good nap?" Tali asked.

Lucas sat up in the hammock.

"I'm fine!" replied Lucas. "I was floating."

Lucy giggled.

"Of course, you're in a hammock," she teased.

"Not just in the hammock," he replied. "I was taken by a bunch of trees to different places I wanted to go," he clarified.

Lucy giggled again.

"What did you have for breakfast?" she asked.

"The same cereal as you," he replied, feeling frustrated. "I'm serious! Something took me and only Paul Bunyan could see me."

Tali came over and handed Lucas some water to drink.

"Take it easy. You have been through

enough this week," she replied calmly.

A few seconds later, Paul Bunyan came tip-toeing carefully through the camp, acting like a two-hundred-foot-tall ninja.

Most campers were out trying to see the President, and no one else even noticed.

Lucas was surprised at how good Paul Bunyan was at moving around unnoticed.

"I saw you!" Paul interrupted, kneeling over the top of a large motor home to get a closer look at Lucas.

Lucy was speechless after finally seeing Paul Bunyan for the first time.

"I saw your shadow and heard your voice. How did you do that?" Paul Bunyan asked.

Lucas smiled as he thought of how he impressed the great Paul Bunyan.

"I don't know," Lucas replied. "The trees did all of the work."

Paul Bunyan reached down and gave Lucas a light push in the hammock with his giant finger.

"You are amazing!" he said proudly. "I need you to teach me how to do that."

Lucas smiled up at him.

"Anytime," he replied.

"How about right now?" asked Paul Bunyan.

"That's fine with me," John Henry interrupted. "We have a few hours before the President returns from Glacier Point."

Paul Bunyan smiled.

"Why don't I give Lucas a quick tour of Yosemite?" Paul suggested.

"Great idea!" Lucas quickly replied. "Can I go?"

Tali moved over so Paul Bunyan could put his hand out to pick Lucas up. Lucy was just standing there in shock, with her mouth open.

"That's a great idea," Tali replied looking up to wink at the friendly giant. "Just take care of my baby."

"Lucy!" Lucas called out, breaking the spell that was over her as she studied the giant man.

"Do you want to come?" Lucas asked.

"I will be just fine right here on the ground," Lucy replied nervously.

Paul Bunyan reached down allowing Lucas to jump into his hand.

"He will be in good hands," Paul said, standing up.

"Wooaahh!" giggled Lucas as the lift into the air tickled his tummy.

Paul Bunyan quickly disappeared across the river past an old hotel. He did not seem worried about being seen.

"Where we going?" asked Lucas.

Paul set Lucas on his shoulder and stood in front of a mountain wall.

"Hold on tight. We need to tell Babe about our meeting by the river, for the Jr. Ranger Celebration," he explained.

"What celebration?" asked Lucas.

"The President has given me a new job as Chief Jr. Ranger, and asked me to accept the job in front of the world as he wants to present me to the world," he explained.

Paul Bunyan took only a couple of minutes to make it to the top of the mountain wall. He started walking towards the Hetch Hetchy Reservoir where Babe, the giant ox was grazing.

"Can I go to the celebration?" Lucas asked.

"Of course, you can. It's right before your family leaves for the Grand Canyon," Paul explained.

Paul took Lucas to the highest point on the mountain, trying to see Babe in the distance.

"Plug your ears little buddy," he warned.

Lucas plugged his ears right before Paul gave one of the loudest whistles ever.

Out in the distance, Lucas heard a faint reply. Babe was letting Paul that he was coming.

It took less than a minute for Lucas to feel the tremble of Babe's footsteps.

"Here he comes," Paul said cheerfully.

It was obvious that he and Babe were best friends.

Lucas spent about an hour showing Paul Bunyan how to connect with the trees.

Paul Bunyan was able to connect, but his connection was limited. It was obvious that Lucas had been chosen to speak for the trees.

Meet the President

The arrival of the President in the Yosemite Valley was an event to be remembered. The sound of several large helicopters thundering through the air unexpectedly sent many unsuspecting tourists running for cover.

Returning from Glacier Point, the First Lady and the President landed in a meadow right across from Yosemite Falls.

Helping his wife and children step out of the helicopter, the President took them on a short hike to see the beautiful waterfall.

Paul Bunyan waited near the waterfall, protected by the President's security team, while John Henry joined the President with his family.

After seeing the falls, they would all return to a meadow in front of the Yosemite Chapel for the President's speech and announcements.

Lucas was full of energy, hiking next to Lucy towards lower Yosemite Falls.

"I can't wait to meet the President," he said to Lucy excitedly.

The President was just ahead of them on the trail, hiking next to his family.

"I doubt he will have time to meet us," Lucy replied.

John and Tali were both listening, right behind them.

"You better think of a question!" Tali said from behind.

"Why?" asked Lucy. "He's too busy."

Tali smiled as she noticed the President on his way over to talk to them.

"This morning he told me that he wanted to meet the both of you in person," Tali explained.

Lucas stopped walking and turned to face his Mom. The group of people behind them all stopped and watched the President sneaking up from behind.

"What could I possibly ask him?" Lucas asked.

Lucy looked at her mom doubtfully.

"Are you serious?" she asked.

Tali ignored her question.

"Try asking him something intelligent," suggested Tali.

Lucy turned around to see where the President was, without seeing him standing right at her side.

"I can't even see him anymore." she said.

"That's because I am right here," the President replied from right next to her.

Lucy laughed thinking it was her dad trying to tease her. She continued walking without even looking at who it was.

"Great impression dad," she said sarcastically.

She was the only one walking.

"How's it going John?" the President said loud enough for Lucy to hear.

"You are still not fooling me," Lucy called back.

Lucas was right in front of the President. "How do you do, Mister President?" he asked politely.

Lucy stopped walking when she noticed the crowd was all turning to watch the President talk to Lucas. She quickly closed her eyes feeling like a dork, wishing she could disappear.

"I am great!" The President replied, shaking Lucas's hand. "I'm surrounded by wonderful people in a beautiful place."

The President was wearing a white

button up long sleeve shirt, rolled up to the elbows, and blue jean pants. Not the usual suit and tie a President normally wears.

"Happy Father's Day!" Lucas said, still catching his breath. He was having a hard time keeping up with the crowd.

The President was impressed at the way Lucas knew exactly what to say, and he was aware of how tired Lucas looked.

"Do you mind if I give you a lift on my shoulders?" the President asked politely.

Lucas gave him a funny look.

"I didn't think a President could do stuff like that," he replied

The President reached down and lifted Lucas up to his shoulders, just like his dad does.

"I do this all the time with my own family." He explained.

Lucas noticed all the guards holding guns and even some had machine guns.

"Why do they have so many guns?" he asked.

The President laughed.

"It's for protection. Many people would try to hurt me or my friends if they could," he explained.

Lucas looked ahead to see a group of kids waiting for the President. Most of them had matching t-shirts.

Someone came over to the President and handed him a stack of plastic cards.

"These are the passes that will allow any fourth grader and their family into a National Park this year," she explained.

The President carefully lifted Lucas back to the ground, holding out the cards to show Lucas.

"These are going to help a lot of families feel welcome in Yosemite, and other parks," he explained. "I will be right back."

The President left Lucas and went straight towards the group of kids, waiting for him. He said a few things and then began handing a card to each of the kids.

His wife came over to help him.

Lucy was now holding John's hand as they came over to Lucas.

"Why doesn't the President have someone else hand out the cards?" Lucy asked her dad.

John smiled.

"He knows that each one of those children is going to remember this moment their entire life. He loves them enough to make sure they feel special," he explained.

"I know I'm going to remember," Lucas said proudly. "He makes me feel like a friend, and we just met."

Lucy was feeling left out a little and was dying to meet him.

"Can we go over there?" she asked.

John held her hand a little tighter.

"You are going to have plenty of time to talk to him. Those kids will only have these few moments to be with him," he explained.

As soon as the President finished, he went right back over to Lucas and Lucy.

"You must be Lucy," he declared.

Lucy's mind went blank and she began to blush.

"Yes I am," she replied. "Are you the President?"

Everyone started to laugh at her question, helping her realize how silly her question was.

"I mean, it's nice to meet you," she clarified.

"I was told you have great ideas," he told Lucy. "What idea do you have to help Yosemite?"

Lucy took a deep breath and thought of the best idea she could give him.

"I think we need to have people take their trash with them when they go home," she suggested.

The President was a little surprised at her amazing suggestion.

"I think we do too!" he replied.

The President called one of his helpers and had him take notes.

When he was finished, he turned back towards Lucy.

"How can we get them to do that?" he asked her.

"Easy," Lucy replied. I bet if you told everyone how cool it is to take the trash with them, they would," she explained.

"I think we can make it cool to take home your trash," he replied.

The President called Lucas over to stand next to Lucy.

"Are you Jr. Ranger's yet?" he asked.

Lucas frowned a little.

"I have been a little busy lately, but all I have left is to pick up trash," he replied.

The President put his finger to his chin.

"That what I'm missing too," he explained.

"Are you trying to become a Jr. ranger?" Lucy asked.

"Of course, I have been working on it all day with my kids," he replied.

He waived for assistance.

"Can we get some trash bags up here!" he shouted.

Suddenly an army of people started moving around trying to find trash bags.

"That will keep them busy until we take a good picture of the waterfall together!" the President said with a smile.

Lucas was excited as he was invited to stand next to the President as the President took a selfie next to Lucas and Lucy.

Tali and John followed as the President spent the next hour walking around with Lucas and Lucy picking up trash, talking about many new ideas needed to help the National Parks.

Jr. Ranger
Celebration

Paul Bunyan was anxious after the President finished his speech and announced his name as the new director of National Jr. Ranger Committee.

Reporters from all over the world were in attendance as hundreds sat in chairs placed in front of the Yosemite Chapel near the meadow. Many children were just waiting to see what Paul Bunyan really looked like.

Paul Bunyan was still hiding, feeling nervous about this moment.

"Dad, get up," Paul Jr. demanded. "We need to get out there!"

Paul Jr. was sitting on his left shoulder next to Lucy holding tightly to his hair.

The President thought it was extremely important that Paul Jr. and the others were seen on his shoulders as he came out from the trees. They would avoid feeling too frightened.

Paul Bunyan finally took a deep breath and walked out from the trees.

"Here we go!" he said.

"They will love you!" Lucas told him right in his ear.

As Paul took a few long steps in-between the trees, he could hear the gasps from the people and children.

Many people stood up to get a better look at him, and several children even screamed, running to sit with their parents.

A video camera zoomed in on Lucas, Lucy, and Paul Jr. to help people feel calm, causing everyone to stand up and cheer.

"You see, they love you, dad!" Paul Jr. said proudly.

"Is that a tear in your eye?" Lucy teased.

Paul Jr. quickly wiped away any evidence.

"No, it's just the wind up here," he replied.

The President spoke into a microphone as he stepped into the middle of Paul Bunyan's hand.

"I present to you, Paul Bunyan, a wonderful man who is going to help lead this country as our Jr. Ranger Director."

Paul Bunyan was comfortable enough to smile and wave to the people.

"Where is Babe?" someone shouted.

Paul began to laugh sending his thunderous voice out into the public for the first time.

Some people ran for cover, but the

majority sat still in their chairs enjoying the greatest moment in Jr. Ranger history.

Paul cleared his voice as the people fell totally silent.

"I am grateful for the opportunity the President has given me to be of service, and I am grateful to be with the people once more, after so many years," he said with a smile.

Many people were clapping for him as he lowered the kids to the ground.

"What do I do next?" he asked the President.

The President smiled.

"I got this!" he replied.

The President walked over to the kids.

"Who wants to go to the river with Paul Bunyan and work on a Jr. Ranger badge?" he called out cheerfully.

Once again, the people began to cheer. Parents began to send their children running towards Paul to follow him to the river.

The President ended the ceremony by

calling loudly into the microphone.

"Let the festivities begin!"

Paul led the children and many parents to the Merced river, only a short walk away. Many kids went swimming while others went fishing. The greatest part of all was when Paul Bunyan would lift the kids and let them jump from his hand like a diving board.

Babe just fell asleep, happy to see his old friend Paul Bunyan with people once more.

After swimming in the river with the Jr. Rangers, the President, and his family said goodbye and climbed into the helicopter.

Before going up the stairs, the President turned back to find Lucy, lifting a bag of trash into the air.

"Hey Lucy," he called. "We are the first ones to show the Love. Taking our trash with us."

Lucy waved goodbye as the President and his family each had a large trash bag to take with them.

Tali and John stood next to Lucy as they watched the helicopter fly away.

"It doesn't get any cooler than this!" Lucy said proudly.

"You did great," Tali told her, giving her a big hug. "Now it's our turn to say goodbye."

Ranger Pam was standing behind Tali holding a large basket from the Yosemite museum. Lucy and Lucas both walked over to say goodbye. Lucy had tears in her eyes.

"I'm going to miss you," she said sadly.

Ranger Pam held up the basket.

"I am going with you," Ranger Pam replied.

Lucy looked up at her, surprised.

"That's great!" Lucy said, immediately cheering up. "What is the basket for?"

"My grandmother made this basket, and we need it for our trip to the Grand Canyon," she replied.

Lucy was thinking of why she would bring such an important basket.

"What do you use it for?" Lucy asked.

Ranger Pam lowered the basket for Lucy to look inside.

"Put your hand inside." Ranger Pam suggested.

Lucy carefully lowered her hand inside, trying to feel what might be inside. She could not even feel the bottom.

"It feels magical," she said. "Why can't I feel the bottom?"

"My Grandmother created this basket to hold the great Kokopelli," she replied.

"Who is the great Kokopelli?" asked Lucy.

"Nowadays we call her Mother Nature," replied Ranger Pam.

Lucy was feeling confused as Lucas interrupted.

"How does Mother Nature fit inside the basket?" he asked. "And how do you plan on catching her?"

Ranger Pam set the basket on the meadow floor, for Lucas to feel inside.

"My ancestors believed that Kokopelli is an

actual person, sent by the Great Spirit," she explained. "She has been provoked and was last seen in the Grand Canyon after causing the Colorado river to dry up.

"She can fit in this basket?" asked Lucas.

"If your father and Pecos Bill can round her up, she will fit inside," Ranger Pam explained.

"Let's go find her," Lucas commanded.

Paul Bunyan looked down at Lucas and Lucy standing next to Ranger Pam and the others.

"I guess we will see you in a few days," he said in a sad voice.

Paul Jr. had the first hug and goodbye, then John tapped Paul on the side of the leg.

"Try and get to the Grand Canyon as fast as you can," he ordered.

"I will see you there," Paul Bunyan replied.

Talitha just blew him a kiss and walked toward the truck with John.

Lucas was like Paul Jr. and hated saying goodbye, even if he knew that he would see

Paul Bunyan in just a few days.

"How do you hug a giant?" Lucas asked.

Paul Bunyan smiled and carefully lifted both Lucas and Lucy up to his heart, pressing them gently against it.

"This is the best I can do," Paul Bunyan replied.

Lucas and Lucy could both feel the love booming from the world's biggest heart, and it was amazing.

Casey Jones

The traffic leaving Yosemite was endless. All the visitors made the drive to Sugar Pine very difficult. It was slow enough that Lucas did not get car sick, and when they finally arrived the sun was already down.

"Where's the train?" asked Lucas.

"It's called the Cannonball," Lucy explained.

Lucas looked back at Lucy making a weird face.

"That a cool name," he replied cheerfully. "Why do they call it that?"

"Because it is faster than an airplane," Lucy replied.

Lucas began to feel worried.

"Are you sure?" he asked.

Paul Jr. was sitting in the front, in-between Tali and John Henry.

"It is quite a bit faster, and it travels under the ground," he explained.

Lucas looked out the window to see if it was out there.

"I can't see it," he protested.

"Hold on Lucas," John insisted. "We always leave at night to avoid being seen."

As soon as John pulled the truck into a loading dock inside a very small train station, everyone finally saw the train. It was pitch black making it almost impossible to see.

"It was here all the time," Lucas said cheerfully. "I have never been on a train."

John looked back at Lucas in the mirror. "There is no other train like the Cannonball," he explained.

146

Lucas was really beginning to get excited.

"What are we waiting for, let's get on the Cannonball," he stated. "It's a beauty!"

Lucy sat up in her seat and took off her seatbelt.

"I'm ready!" she announced.

Unexpectedly, all of the train lights turned on and the sound of the horn exploded full blast.

Everyone except John was forced to plug their ears.

"What was that for? Can't he see us here?" she asked.

"Casey is just running tests in there to make sure the Cannonball will run smoothly," John explained.

"Who made it go so fast?" asked Lucas.

John was happy to tell.

"I helped set up the tracks and dug the underground passages. It was Granville Woods and Elijah McCoy who worked with Casey Jones to bring the Cannonball to life," he explained.

"Do we get to meet them also?" asked Lucas.

John gave the question some thought before giving his reply.

"Probably not on this trip, but soon," he replied happily. "They will show you things they invented that will make you proud."

After a few minutes, everyone was out of the truck and waiting for Casey Jones to welcome them on the train.

"Who do we have here?" a friendly voice called from inside.

A man almost as tall as John Henry came out of the train door to welcome everyone. He was wearing a tall blue hat that matched a pair of perfectly clean blue overalls. His shirt looked like it had been made by the same tailor as Paul Bunyan.

John was the first to step forward giving him a big hug.

"It has been a long time old friend," he said patting him on the back.

"It sure has," Casey replied, looking around at the rest of the group. "Who did you bring with you?"

Paul Jr. immediately took Casey's hand and began shaking it. Casey was amused.

"Paul Jr. here, reporting for my trip to Ireland," he explained.

Lucas interrupted.

"We're not going to Ireland. We are going to find Kokopelli in the Grand Canyon," he said firmly.

Lucy smiled.

"Don't mind my brother Lucas, he gets excited about the strangest things," she explained.

"You both must be the ESP twins that were adopted by John and Talitha," Casey said greeting them onto the train.

"I hear Paul Bunyan will meet us there," he said looking at John.

"That is correct," John replied.

"Then welcome aboard, one and all!" Casey

shouted.

Ranger Pam was standing in the corner of the room.

"I don't think we have met before," Casey said in his romantic voice.

Lucy covered her mouth almost blushing.

"Someone has a crush," she whispered to Paul Jr. and Lucas.

Ranger Pam held her grandmother's basket in her arms.

"I am Pamahas, and stop acting like we have never met," she replied.

"Are you coming with us?" Casey asked.

It was the first time Lucy had ever seen someone make Ranger Pam blush.

Ranger Pam lifted the basket so that he could see it.

"I am the only person who can work the basket that will hold Kokopelli," she explained.

"That sounds like a great reason to have you with us," Casey replied, looking ready to take off.

"Enough fun for today," he said with an Irish accent. "Allllll aboard!"

It only took a few minutes until Casey Jones and John Henry had everyone loaded in the beautiful caboose of the Cannonball. Each sitting in the most comfortable velvet chairs.

The truck full of camping gear was loaded soon after.

Casey found Lucas with something important to tell him.

"Hi Casey, are we leaving now?" Lucas asked.

"Are you ready to see some dinosaurs?" Casey asked suspiciously.

Lucas immediately felt nervous, looking over at John to see how far away he was.

"No," Lucas replied nervously. "I did not come to see dinosaurs."

Casey began to laugh.

"Good, because the Cannonball can't time travel yet," he explained with a grin.

"That's good," Lucas replied.

Everyone put on their seatbelt, sitting back in the chairs as Casey Jones took the Cannonball to full speed. The Cannonball immediately entered a tunnel that went deep into the Earth's crust, beginning their journey to the Grand Canyon.

Fun and Games

*word search *
new pictures
trivia
and more

Historic Yosemite Names

```
R E N G P N V V L Z T I E J S
O H E X A F C V P P Y L K N E
O F V N R L E Z N G E L I E D
S X Y O H P E Z U H A K C N C
E O A R H A N N S D T M L O N
V L H C H M W N C A P K F C R
E E I H T I X H W L O P A Z O
L T Q I F Z X N A W A M A Y M
T N E V F J O R I I P R V I O
T N R J W T A M C C U U K X M
S F J F E J Q V U V X E E C Q
X I S L U K D R P P E T Q R W
E M R C Y B R T Q M J U G B V
Q A R D N Y V N R B B I S U W
C L A R E H O D G E S A N Z N
Q S A R I U M N H O J P Q U Y
```

AHWAHNEE   CAMPCURRY
CARLETONWATKINS
CLAREHODGES   GALENCLARK
JOHNMUIR   MIWOK
PAIUTE   ROOSEVELT

154

Fun Fact

The word Ahwahnee comes from the Ahwahnechee people who lived in the Yosemite Valley for thousands of years.

Ahwahnee, meaning "the valley shaped like a big mouth"

Jr Ranger Adventure
Folk Heroes

```
J S P P G I J D I X E Q W O J
F L E P E C P L M L G I U O P
X K L N Z C L X M B Y L H Y T
E T W M O E O E I M E N C R B
W K I Q P J R S M A N U Z N U
I A V O V Q Y E B Y J N B E T
Q V K V O V R E A I F A F H O
V O R S Y G Y P S P L J X N L
K E K N Y X P F P A V L H H U
Y W S Z I L S K B O C U I O C
K R E Z E C A I H E V S V J Y
V I B S L U C A S F E R N J F
M V E V V H D Q D D M K V J E
E E I N A Y N U B L U A P J R
D G B F F K V J R Q T F J U N
```

CASEYJONES   ELMER
JOHNHENRY   JOHNNYAPPLESEED
KOKOPELLI   LUCASFERN
LUCYFERN   PAULBUNYAN
PECOS BILL

Fun Fact

The Merced River is the largest river running through the Yosemite Valley. It was named by Spanish colonists in the 1800s' They named the river "Rio de Nuestra Señora de la Merced (River of Our Lady of Mercy)"

Great Hikes in Yosemite

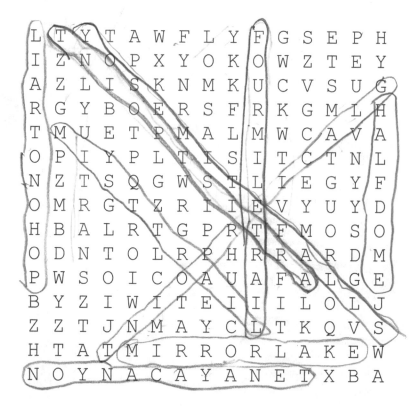

```
L T Y T A W F L Y F G S E P H
I Z N O P X Y O K O W Z T E Y
A Z L I S K N M K U C V S U G
R G Y B O E R S F R K G M L H
T M U E T P M A L M W C A V A
O P I Y P L T I S I T C T N L
N Z T S Q G W S T L I E G Y F
O M R G T Z R I I E V Y U Y D
H B A L R T G P R T F M O S O
O D N T O L R P H R R A R D M
P W S O I C O A U A F A L G E
B Y Z I W I T E I I I L O L J
Z Z T J N M A Y C L T K Q V S
H T A T M I R R O R L A K E W
N O Y N A C A Y A N E T X B A
```

ARTISTPOINT   FOURMILETRAIL
GLACIERPOINT   HALFDOME
MIRRORLAKE   MISTTRAIL
POHONOTRAIL   TENAYACANYON
YOSEMITEFALLS

Fun Fact

The name of Yosemite is related to the
Sierra Miwok word
for (grizzly) bear
Grizzly bears were common in Yosemite
and California before the discovery of
gold.

Sad Fact

California laws in the 1800's allowed Grizzly
bears to be hunted and killed in California.
In 1866, one of the last grizzly bears in
California, described as weighing as much as
2,200 pounds was killed in Valley Center,
California
Yosemite is pronounced yo-SE-mea-tea.
Ahwahnee is pronounced ah-WAA-nee.

Popular Animals of Yosemite

P X D M B C R D Y Y V A M N R
A U A Q U N K D Z X L O R O E
C R O R S L S W L J U Y Y R D
I Z T K F Y E Z Y N F A B O F
F S E Q X I Z D T E J A K U O
I W T U Z X F A E S T F N X X
C Q I W Y U I V R E D D S V A
F Z M U W N D E T C R J W Q X
I W E M L B L A C K B E A R M
S I S I V L D C X C O J T Y F
H Y O P E E H S N R O H G I B
E N Y T S I S A Z D M L X D O
R A S T V X E I P O O E F N L
N O M T G O A V F I Z F P U C
S V D Y R Q A A R B N E H H X

BAT   BIGHORNSHEEP
BLACKBEAR   MOUNTAINLION
MULEDEER   PACIFICFISHER
REDFOX   STELLERSJAY
YOSEMITETOAD

160

Fun Fact

Yosemite has approximately 90 mammal species and mule deer are especially common. More injuries in Yosemite are inflicted by deer, with one documented death, than by black bear or any other park animal.

Bear cubs can also be common so Remember to never pet the animals!

Fun things to do in Yosemite

```
O M Y Y G V C A S H Y G K K T
X C D E W E K I H K S X C F X
K Z V L G K S P N B I O A B Z
B I K E G T T M W D R R Q L V
M C H F K Z A A D A Y B G N X
C I N N J H O C B Y R W N C J
I M W P E M M M X S W N L L Z
N C N S E W I T J F H I F V T
C Q E V O L U N T E E R I O S
G O G S S S J A G I I F S T R
R C Q V K D K P U S C I H W P
L K M I A A S A K V J F I W I
W W V S A S T A M S Q J N K S
P V C O K O T E V U P Q G X X
R J Z C E E Z Y B Z R T F X W
```

BIKE   CAMP   CLIMBAROCK

FISHING   HIKE   ICESKATE

NAP   RAFT   SKATE

SKI   SWIM   VOLUNTEER

Sad Fact

Between 20-30 bears are killed a year by speeding drivers in Yosemite.

Are you driving the speed limit?

Most bears in Southern California including Big Bear are descendants of the Yosemite Black Bear.

In 1933 the mountain lion population was getting out of hand in Big Bear so authorities brought black bears from Yosemite to Big Bear to help balance out the predator population.

Fun Fact

Yosemite is a very safe place to camp!

Even with black bears and other animals around, if you store your food properly and put your trash inside the large metal dumpsters, you will not be bothered.

A black bear's diet consists mainly of berries, grasses, nuts, and insects. Black bears are naturally shy of humans.

Please read our Next Book in the Jr. Ranger Series where John Henry looks for Kokopelli in the Grand Canyon.

Also, here is our first Lucas Fern book.
Lucas and Lucy move to a new home
near the oldest tree on the planet. The
Old Hara tree.

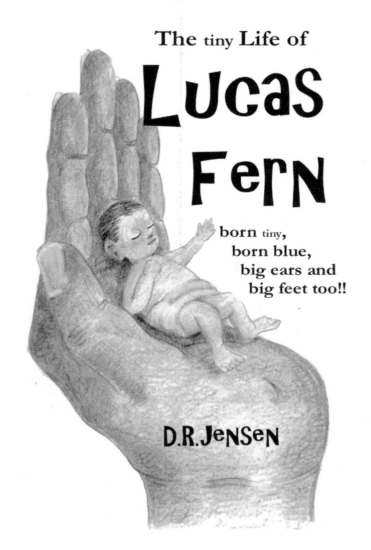

The tiny Life of

Lucas
Fern

born tiny,
born blue,
big ears and
big feet too!!

D.R.Jensen

all books by Derek Ryan Jensen

The tiny Life of Lucas Fern (published 2016)
Paul Bunyan & me in Yosemite (published 2017)

Almost Finished:
John Henry & Me in the Grand Canyon (spring/summer
2017)

Coming Soon:
Lucy Fern "What's in a Name?"
with co/Author
(daughter) Adriana Jensen (Summer 2017)
Saint Nicholas & Me (fall 2017)

Possible National Park Titles coming in 2018 & 2019

Wicklow Mountains National Park (Ireland)
Smoky Mountains
Yellowstone
Kamikochi (Japan)
Jiuzhai Valley (China)
Stolby National Park (Russia)
New Forest National Park (England)

Connect with Author
Derek Ryan Jensen

www.derekryanjensen.com

www.lucasfern.com